CGP are in the top division for Maths!

This CGP book quickly gets pupils up to speed with the Multiplication and Division skills they need for Year 5.

Each test only takes 10 minutes, so they're ideal for quick practice sessions — and we've carefully crafted each one to get more difficult as pupils build up their confidence.

We've even included step-by-step answers to every question — plus a handy chart to check progress too!

What CGP is all about

Our sole aim here at CGP is to produce the highest quality books — carefully written, immaculately presented and dangerously close to being funny.

Then we work our socks off to get them out to you — at the cheapest possible prices.

Published by CGP

Editors: Laura Collins, Liam Dyer, Samuel Mann, Sean McParland and Caley Simpson.

With thanks to Shaun Harrogate, Joanne Haslett and Gareth Mitchell for the proofreading.

With thanks to Jan Greenway for the copyright research.

ISBN: 978 1 78908 647 8

Clipart from Corel®
Printed by Zenith Print & Packaging Ltd, Pontypridd.

Based on the classic CGP style created by Richard Parsons.

Text, design, layout and original illustrations © Coordination Group Publications Ltd. (CGP) 2020
All rights reserved.

Photocopying this book is not permitted, even if you have a CLA licence.
Extra copies are available from CGP with next day delivery • 0800 1712 712 • www.cgpbooks.co.uk

Contents

Test 1 2
Test 2 4
Test 3 6
Test 4 8
Test 5 10
Test 6 12
Test 7 14
Test 8 16
Test 9 18
Test 10 20
Test 11 22
Test 12 24
Answers 26
Progress Chart 30

How to Use this Book

- This book contains 12 tests, all geared towards improving your multiplication and division skills.

- Each test is out of 11 marks and should take about 10 minutes to complete.

- Each test starts with some warm-up questions to get you going and ends with a problem-solving question.

- The tests increase in difficulty as you go through the book.

- Answers and a Progress Chart can be found at the back of the book.

Test 1

Warm up

1. Use your times tables to calculate:

   a) 6 × 3 = ...

   b) 3 × 5 = ...

   c) 9 × 4 = ...

   d) 7 × 8 = ...

   2 marks

2. Fill in the gaps to complete these calculations.

   a) 9 × .... = 9

   b) 7 × 0 = ...

   c) .... × 20 = 20

   d) 15 × .... = 0

   2 marks

3. Draw lines to match each calculation with its answer.

   | 11 × 4 | 9 × 4 | 12 × 12 | 6 × 7 |

   | 144 | 44 | 42 | 36 |

   2 marks

4. Use the calculation below to work out 18 × 30.

   18 × 3 = 54

   ....

   1 mark

5. Work out the answers to these calculations.

```
   2 7         3 2         2 9
×    3       ×   5       ×   6
-----        -----        -----
.......      .......      .......
```

2 marks

6. Alison is catching monsters in a video game.
Each monster scores a certain number of points, as shown below.

Dragon	80 points
Troll	35 points
Goblin	12 points

Alison catches one dragon, two trolls and four goblins.

How many points does she score?

.... points

2 marks

END OF TEST

/ 11

Test 2

Warm up

1. Fill in the gaps to complete these calculations.

   a) 3 × .... = 24 b) .... × 7 = 49

   c) 6 × .... = 66 d) .... × 8 = 72

   2 marks

2. Work out the answer to each of these calculations.

   a) 20 ÷ 4 = ... b) 70 ÷ 10 = ...

   c) 27 ÷ 3 = ... d) 64 ÷ 8 = ...

   2 marks

3. Circle the number sentence below that is true.

   8 ÷ 4 = 4 ÷ 8   4 × 8 = 8 × 4   8 ÷ 4 = 4 × 8

   1 mark

4. Write in the missing digits to make these calculations correct.

   ```
       2 ☐              ☐ 5
   ×     3          ×     7
   ─────            ─────
     ☐ 8              2 4 ☐
       1                  3
   ```

   2 marks

5. Work out:

2 × 5 × 3 = ...   6 × 2 × 10 = ...

1 mark

6. What is 68 × 6?

....

1 mark

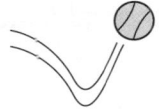

7. A sports shop sells tubes of tennis balls.
Each tube contains 5 yellow balls and 4 blue balls.

Moe buys enough tubes to have 81 tennis balls in total.

How many of the 81 balls are yellow?

.... yellow balls

2 marks

END OF TEST

/ 11

Test 3

Warm up

1. a) Circle all the multiples of 6:   16   26   36   46   66

    b) Circle all the multiples of 7:   14   27   42   67   73

    _____
    1 mark

2. Use your times tables to work out these calculations.

    a) 3 × 20 = ...   b) 4 × 30 = ...

    c) 6 × 50 = ...   d) 11 × 30 = ...

    _____
    2 marks

3. Circle all the calculations that have an answer of 4.

    16 ÷ 4   24 ÷ 8   48 ÷ 6

           36 ÷ 9   36 ÷ 12   28 ÷ 7

    _____
    1 mark

4. Work out:

    14 × 10 = ...   370 × 10 = ...

    20 × 100 = ...   85 × 1000 = ...

    _____
    2 marks

5. Work out the answers to these calculations.

```
    2 4 3              4 1 5
  ×     3            ×     4
  ───────            ───────

  ...........        ...........
```
2 marks

6. Simrat finds 72 ants and 56 spiders in her garden. Ants have six legs and spiders have eight legs.

   She works out how many legs the ants have in total using the method below.

   Fill in the gaps in Simrat's working.

   $72 × 6 = \boxed{} × 6 + 2 × 6 = \boxed{} + 12 = \boxed{}$ legs

   1 mark

   Use Simrat's method to work out how many legs the spiders have in total.

   .... legs

   2 marks

END OF TEST

/ 11

Test 4

Warm up

1. Fill in the gaps to complete these calculations.

    a) 11 × 9 = ...
    b) 6 × .... = 48
    c) 7 × .... = 35
    d) .... × 12 = 120

    2 marks

2. Circle the calculations where the missing number is 1.

    5 × ? = 0   15 ÷ ? = 15   20 × ? = 20   10 ÷ ? = 1

    1 mark

3. Tick the correct box next to each number sentence to show whether it is true or false.

    2 × 12 = 4 × 8   True ☐   False ☐

    40 ÷ 5 = 88 ÷ 11   True ☐   False ☐

    4 × 3 = 64 ÷ 8   True ☐   False ☐

    2 marks

4. Work out the answers to these calculations.

    0.7 × 10 = ...   0.39 × 100 = ...

    5.2 × 100 = ...   8.15 × 1000 = ...

    2 marks

5. Work out:

Forty-six multiplied by seven

....
1 mark

Eight multiplied by seventy-nine

....
1 mark

6. A school canteen sells two types of fruit.

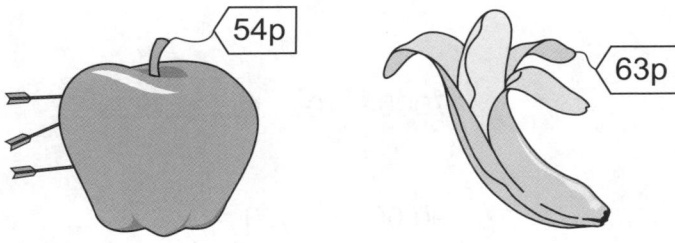

Harry and his four friends buy one apple and one banana **each**.

How much do Harry and his friends spend in total?

£ ....
2 marks

END OF TEST

/ 11

Test 5

Warm up

1. Use your times tables to calculate:

   a) 56 ÷ 8 = ...   b) 36 ÷ 9 = ...

   c) 42 ÷ 7 = ...   d) 121 ÷ 11 = ...

   2 marks

2. Circle all the numbers below that are factors of 24.

       1   3   5   9   12   18

   1 mark

3. Work out:

   830 ÷ 10 = ...   7000 ÷ 10 = ...

   4600 ÷ 100 = ...   90 000 ÷ 1000 = ...

   2 marks

4. Fill in the boxes to complete these calculations.

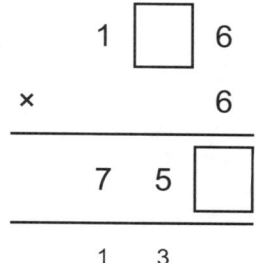
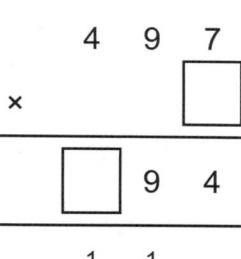
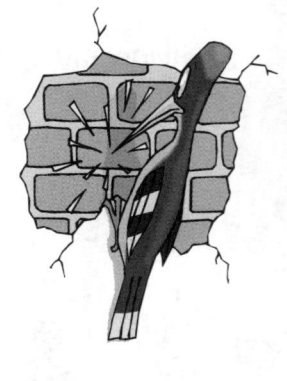

2 marks

5. Work out the answers to these calculations.

   3) 9 3   5) 6 5   7) 9 8

   2 marks

6. A maths magician asks a member of his audience to pick three of the cards below.

They pick the three cards that show multiples of 4. The magician multiplies all three numbers together.

What number does the magician get?

2 marks

END OF TEST

/ 11

Test 6

Warm up

1. Fill in the gaps to complete these calculations.

   a) .... × 10 = 740

   b) 10 × .... = 800

   1 mark

2. Use your times tables to work out these calculations.

   a) 360 ÷ 4 = ...

   b) 480 ÷ 80 = ...

   c) 400 ÷ 5 = ...

   d) 5400 ÷ 90 = ...

   2 marks

3. Work out:

   365 × 4

   286 × 7

   ....

   ....

   2 marks

4. Draw lines to match each calculation with its answer.

   | 0.24 ÷ 10 | 2400 ÷ 100 | 2.4 ÷ 10 | 240 ÷ 100 |

   | 2.4 | 0.24 | 0.024 | 24 |

   1 mark

5. What is eight lots of two hundred and eleven?

....
1 mark

6. Work out the answers to these calculations.

```
  2 3 3 4              3 6 0 5
×       3            ×       5
---------            ---------
```

....
2 marks

7. Celia is given £90 for her birthday.

She spends £12 on a yoga mat and the rest of her money on books. Each book costs £6.

How many books does she buy?

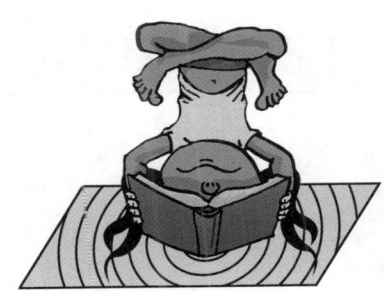

.... books
2 marks

END OF TEST

/ 11

Test 7

Warm up

1. Fill in the gaps to complete these calculations.

   a) 11 × 11 = ...   b) .... × 9 = 81

   c) 9 × .... = 63   d) 12 × 8 = ...

   2 marks

2. Circle three numbers below that multiply together to give 42.

   2   3   4   5   6   7   8

   1 mark

3. Using one number from each box, write one multiplication and one division that both have the answer 46.

   | 0.46   4.6   46   460   4600 | | 10   100   1000 |

   .... ÷ .... = 46

   .... × .... = 46

   1 mark

4. Work out these calculations. Give your answers in numbers.

   sixty-eight multiplied by one hundred = ...

   ninety-seven multiplied by one thousand = ...

   2 marks

5. Work out the answers to these calculations.

    .... remainder: .... remainder: ......
    8 | 9 2   7 | 8 5

    2 marks

6. Fill in the boxes to complete this calculation.

    ```
              2   5
        ×     1   4
        ─────────────
          1   0₂  0
    +   ☐   ☐   ☐
        ─────────────
        ☐   ☐   ☐
    ```

    1 mark

7. A box of fishing bait costs 80p.
    Bobby can catch 7 fish using one box of fishing bait.

    How much will he need to spend on fishing bait
    if he wants to catch at least 40 fish?

    £....................

    2 marks

END OF TEST

/ 11

Test 8

Warm up

1. Circle all the square numbers in the list below:

   2   4   10   15   25   35

   1 mark

2. Complete these calculations.

   a) 58 × .... = 580

   b) 14 × .... = 1400

   c) 7400 ÷ .... = 740

   d) 2600 ÷ .... = 26

   2 marks

3. Work out the answers to these calculations.

   ```
       1 2 3 4              2 5 1 4
   ×         6          ×         8
   ─────────              ─────────
   ```

   ....

   2 marks

4. Work out:

   .... remainder: .... remainder: ......

   3 | 5 6 2   6 | 6 9 9

   2 marks

Test 8   16   © CGP — not to be photocopied

5. A teacher divides 97 worksheets equally between seven pupils.

   How many worksheets does each pupil get?
   How many are left over?

   .... worksheets

   .... left over

   2 marks

6. A farmer has 156 sheep. He buys 51 more sheep.
   One pen will hold 9 sheep.

   How many pens will he need to hold all of the sheep?

   .... pens

   2 marks

END OF TEST

/ 11

Test 9

Warm up

1. a) Circle all the multiples of 9:   18   26   39   45   58

    b) Circle all the multiples of 12:   22   36   52   60   72

    2 marks

2. Use your times tables to complete these calculations.

    a) 3 × .... = 240

    b) .... × 40 = 160

    c) .... × 6 = 4200

    d) 80 × .... = 7200

    2 marks

3. Label each stage of the number machine below with the correct multiplication or division.

    0.81 → .... → 810 → .... → 8.1

    1 mark

4. Work out the answers to these calculations.

    ```
      4 2 1 9            3 2 0 3
    ×       5          ×       7
    ─────────          ─────────
    ```

    ....

    2 marks

5. Find the remainder when:

   568 is divided by 3   846 is divided by 7

   Remainder: ....   Remainder: ....

   2 marks

6. 182 people need to travel home from a wedding.

   Each bus holds   Each taxi holds
   48 people   4 people

   Three buses are filled and everyone else travels by taxi.

   What is the **smallest** number of taxis needed so that everyone can travel home from the wedding?

   .... taxis

   2 marks

END OF TEST

/ 11

Test 10

Warm up

1. Use your times tables to work out these calculations.

   a) 60 × 9 = ...
   b) 70 × 70 = ...
   c) 11 × 80 = ...
   d) 50 × 120 = ...

   2 marks

2. Work out the answers to these calculations.

   a) 3 × 3 × 7 = ...
   b) 12 × 1 × 4 = ...

   1 mark

3. Work out:

   27 × 23   39 × 26

   ....

   2 marks

4. Work out the answers to these calculations.

   ```
       2 8 2              4 2 2
   ×     3 1          ×     4 3
   ───────────        ───────────
   ```

   2 marks

Test 10

Progress Chart

That's all the tests in the book done — nice one!

Now fill in this table with all of your scores and see how you got on.

	Score
Test 1	
Test 2	
Test 3	
Test 4	
Test 5	
Test 6	
Test 7	
Test 8	
Test 9	
Test 10	
Test 11	
Test 12	

4.
```
     2 8 2              4 2 2
   ×   3 1            ×   4 3
     2 8 2            1 2 6 6
  + 8₂4 6 0         +1 6 8 8 0
    8 7 4 2  (1 mark)  1 8 1 4 6  (1 mark)
      1                  1 1
```

5. Divide the number of roses by 6:
```
      1 4 8 r 3
   6 | 8 ²9 ⁵1
```
She makes equal bunches, so ignore the remainder. So she makes 148 whole bunches. **(1 mark)**

Divide the number of tulips by 7:
```
      1 2 9 r 6
   7 | 9 ²0 ⁶9
```
She will have 129 full vases and 1 vase of 6 tulips. So she needs 130 vases. **(1 mark)**

6. Work backwards through the machine. The last step was to multiply by 6, so first divide 864 by 6:
```
      1 4 4
   6 | 8 ²6 ²4   (1 mark)
```
So 144 is equal to the square of the number she put into the machine. 144 = 12², so she put 12 into the machine. **(1 mark)**

Test 11 – pages 22-23

1. a) 8   b) 64
   (1 mark for both correct)

2. a) 11   b) 10   c) 20   d) 2
   (2 marks for all four correct, otherwise 1 mark for at least two correct)

3.
```
      0 1 5 4 remainder: 3
   7 | 1 ¹0 ³8 ³1                (1 mark)
      1 5 7 7 remainder: 2
   3 | 4 ¹7 ²3 ²3                (1 mark)
```

4.
```
       9 3                 6 7
     ×   2 4             ×   4 9
       3 7₁2               6 0₆3
     +1 8 6 0            + 2 6₂8 0
       2 2 3 2 (1 mark)    3 2 8 3  (1 mark)
         1 1                   1
```

5.
```
       3 0 2 7              4 3 1 1
     ×     2 1            ×     1 8
       3 0 2 7            3 4₂4 8 8
    + 6 0 5₁4 0         + 4 3 1 1 0
      6 3 5 6 7 (1 mark)   7 7 5 9 8 (1 mark)
```

6. Multiply 135 by 9 to find the amount of flour he needs for nine servings:
```
       1 3 5
     ×     9
       1 2 1 5
         3 4
```
So he needs 1215 g of flour in total.
1 kg = 1000 g of flour, so he needs
1215 – 1000 = 215 g more flour.
(2 marks for the correct answer, otherwise 1 mark for a correct method)

Test 12 – pages 24-25

1. a) 6   b) 720   c) 40
   (2 marks for all three correct, otherwise 1 mark for two correct)

2. a) 1000   b) 7.84   c) 122   d) 1000
   (2 marks for all four correct, otherwise 1 mark for at least two correct)

3.
```
       2 0 4               8 6 1
     ×   3 6             ×   9 2
      1 2 2₂4             1 7₁2 2
     +6 1₁2 0            +7 7₅4 9 0
      7 3 4 4  (1 mark)   7 9 2 1 2  (1 mark)
                              1 1
```

4. Divide the number of eggs by 6:
```
      0 2 2 4 r 2
   6 | 1 ¹3 ¹4 ²6
```
So she fills 224 boxes. **(1 mark)**

5.
```
       3 1 0 6              4 2 8 8
     ×     4 2            ×     1 7
       6 2 1₁2             3 0₂0₆1₅6
     +1 2 4 2₂4 0         +4 2 8 8 0
      1 3 0 4 5 2 (1 mark)  7 2 8 9 6  (1 mark)
            1
```

6. The side length of the cube is 12 cm, so first do 12 × 12 = 144. Then work out 144 × 12:
```
       1 4 4
     ×   1 2
       2 8 8
     +1 4 4 0
       1 7 2 8
         1
```
So the volume of the cube is 1728 cm³.
(2 marks for the correct answer, otherwise 1 mark for a correct method)

4. 68 × 100 = 6800 (**1 mark**)
   97 × 1000 = 97 000 (**1 mark**)
5.
   $$8 \overline{)9\,^1 2} \quad \begin{array}{l} 1\ 1\ \text{remainder: 4} \end{array}$$
   (**1 mark**)

   $$7 \overline{)8\,^1 5} \quad \begin{array}{l} 1\ 2\ \text{remainder: 1} \end{array}$$
   (**1 mark**)
6.
   ```
       2 5
     ×  1 4
     ─────
     1 0₂0
     + 2 5 0
     ─────
     3 5 0
   ```
   (**1 mark**)
7. Bobby can catch 5 × 7 = 35 fish from 5 boxes of fishing bait. This is less than 40.
   He can catch 6 × 7 = 42 fish from 6 boxes.
   So he needs 6 boxes. 6 boxes of fishing bait will cost 6 × 80p = 480p = £4.80.
   (**2 marks for the correct answer, otherwise 1 mark for a correct method**)

Test 8 – pages 16-17

1. 4 and 25 should be circled. (**1 mark**)
2. a) 10   b) 100   c) 10   d) 100
   (**2 marks for all four correct, otherwise 1 mark for at least two correct**)
3.
   ```
       1 2 3 4              2 5 1 4
     ×       6            ×       8
     ─────────            ─────────
       7 4 0 4              2 0 1 1 2
         1 2 2                  4 1 3
   ```
   (**1 mark**) (**1 mark**)
4.
   $$3 \overline{)5\,^2 6\,^2 2} \quad \begin{array}{l} 1\ 8\ 7\ \text{remainder: 1} \end{array}$$
   (**1 mark**)

   $$6 \overline{)6\ 9\,^3 9} \quad \begin{array}{l} 1\ 1\ 6\ \text{remainder: 3} \end{array}$$
   (**1 mark**)
5.
   $$7 \overline{)9\,^2 7} \quad \begin{array}{l} 1\ 3\ \text{remainder 6} \end{array}$$
   So each pupil gets 13 worksheets and there are 6 left over.
   (**1 mark for the correct number of worksheets for each pupil, 1 mark for the correct number left over**)
6. The farmer has 156 + 51 = 207 sheep, so divide 207 by 9:

   $$9 \overline{)2\,^2 0\,^2 7} \quad \begin{array}{l} 2\ 3 \end{array}$$
   So he will need 23 pens.
   (**2 marks for the correct answer, otherwise 1 mark for a correct method**)

Test 9 – pages 18-19

1. a) 18 and 45 should be circled. (**1 mark**)
   b) 36, 60 and 72 should be circled. (**1 mark**)
2. a) 80   b) 4   c) 700   d) 90
   (**2 marks for all four correct, otherwise 1 mark for at least two correct**)
3. 0.81 × 1000 = 810, 810 ÷ 100 = 8.1
   So the two boxes on the number machine should be labelled '× 1000' and '÷ 100'.
   (**1 mark for both correct**)
4.
   ```
       4 2 1 9              3 2 0 3
     ×       5            ×       7
     ─────────            ─────────
     2 1 0 9 5            2 2 4 2 1
         1 4                  1 2
   ```
   (**1 mark**) (**1 mark**)
5.
   $$3 \overline{)5\,^2 6\,^2 8} \quad \begin{array}{l} 1\ 8\ 9\ \text{remainder: 1} \end{array}$$
   (**1 mark**)

   $$7 \overline{)8\,^1 4\ 6} \quad \begin{array}{l} 1\ 2\ 0\ \text{remainder: 6} \end{array}$$
   (**1 mark**)
6. Do 48 × 3 to find the number of people in three full buses:
   ```
       4 8
     ×   3
     ─────
     1 4 4
         2
   ```
   So 182 – 144 = 38 people need taxis.
   38 ÷ 4 = 9 r 2. 9 taxis would not be enough as there would be 2 people left behind, so the smallest number of taxis needed is 10.
   (**2 marks for the correct answer, otherwise 1 mark for a correct method**)

Test 10 – pages 20-21

1. a) 540   b) 4900
   c) 880   d) 6000
   (**2 marks for all four correct, otherwise 1 mark for at least two correct**)
2. a) 63   b) 48
   (**1 mark for both correct**)
3.
   ```
         2 7                    3 9
       × 2 3                  × 2 6
       ─────                  ─────
         8₂1                  2 3₅4
     + 5₁4 0                + 7₁8 0
       ─────                  ─────
       6 2 1                  1 0 1 4
         1                        1
   ```
   (**1 mark**) (**1 mark**)

Test 4 – pages 8-9

1. a) 99 b) 8 c) 5 d) 10
   (**2 marks for all four correct,
   otherwise 1 mark for at least two correct**)
2. 15 ÷ 1 = 15 and 20 × 1 = 20 should be circled.
   (**1 mark**)
3. 2 × 12 = 24 and 4 × 8 = 32, so it's false.
   40 ÷ 5 = 8 and 88 ÷ 11 = 8, so it's true.
   4 × 3 = 12 and 64 ÷ 8 = 8, so it's false.
   (**2 marks for all three correct,
   otherwise 1 mark for two correct**)
4. 0.7 × 10 = 7   0.39 × 100 = 39
   5.2 × 100 = 520   8.15 × 1000 = 8150
   (**2 marks for all four correct,
   otherwise 1 mark for at least two correct**)
5.
   ```
     4 6            7 9
   ×   7          ×   8
   -----          -----
   3 2 2 (1 mark) 6 3 2 (1 mark)
     4                7
   ```
6. One apple and one banana costs
   54p + 63p = 117p. There are five
   people in total, so do 117 × 5:
   ```
     1 1 7
   ×     5
   -------
     5 8 5
         3
   ```
   So they spend 585p = £5.85 in total.
   (**2 marks for the correct answer,
   otherwise 1 mark for a correct method**)

Test 5 – pages 10-11

1. a) 7 b) 4 c) 6 d) 11
   (**2 marks for all four correct,
   otherwise 1 mark for at least two correct**)
2. 1, 3 and 12 should be circled. (**1 mark**)
3. 830 ÷ 10 = 83   7000 ÷ 10 = 700
   4600 ÷ 100 = 46   90 000 ÷ 1000 = 90
   (**2 marks for all four correct,
   otherwise 1 mark for at least two correct**)
4.
   ```
     1 2 6             4 9 7
   ×     6           ×     2
   -------           -------
     7 5 6 (1 mark)    9 9 4 (1 mark)
       1 3                 1 1
   ```
5.
   ```
       3 1            1 3            1 4
   3 ) 9 3        5 ) 6 ¹5       7 ) 9 ²8
   ```
   (**2 marks for all three correct,
   otherwise 1 mark for two correct**)

6. The three multiples of 4 are 36, 4 and 8.
   Multiply two numbers together then multiply
   the answer by the third number:
   ```
     3 6              1 4 4
   ×   4            ×     8
   -----            -------
   1 4 4            1 1 5 2
     2                3 3
   ```
   So the magician gets the number 1152.
   (**2 marks for the correct answer,
   otherwise 1 mark for a correct method**)

Test 6 – pages 12-13

1. a) 74 b) 80 (**1 mark for both correct**)
2. a) 90 b) 6 c) 80 d) 60
   (**2 marks for all four correct,
   otherwise 1 mark for at least two correct**)
3.
   ```
     3 6 5              2 8 6
   ×     4            ×     7
   -------            -------
   1 4 6 0 (1 mark)   2 0 0 2 (1 mark)
     2 2                6 4
   ```
4.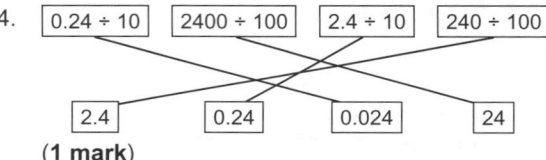
   (**1 mark**)
5.
   ```
     2 1 1
   ×     8
   -------
   1 6 8 8 (1 mark)
   ```
6.
   ```
     2 3 3 4              3 6 0 5
   ×       3            ×       5
   ---------            ---------
     7 0 0 2 (1 mark)   1 8 0 2 5 (1 mark)
     1 1 1                  3 2
   ```
7. £90 – £12 = £78
   ```
       1 3
   6 ) 7 ¹8        So she buys 13 books.
   ```
   (**2 marks for the correct answer,
   otherwise 1 mark for a correct method**)

Test 7 – pages 14-15

1. a) 121 b) 9 c) 7 d) 96
   (**2 marks for all four correct,
   otherwise 1 mark for at least two correct**)
2. 2, 3 and 7 should be circled. (**1 mark**)
3. 4600 ÷ 100 = 46 or 460 ÷ 10 = 46
   0.46 × 100 = 46 or 4.6 × 10 = 46
   (**1 mark for both correct**)

Answers

Test 1 – pages 2-3

1. a) 18 b) 15 c) 36 d) 56
   (2 marks for all four correct, otherwise 1 mark for at least two correct)
2. a) 1 b) 0 c) 1 d) 0
   (2 marks for all four correct, otherwise 1 mark for at least two correct)
3.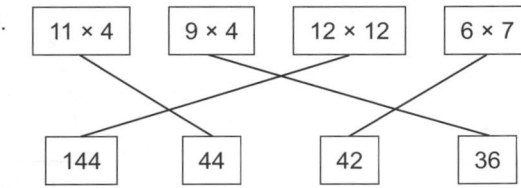
   (2 marks for all lines drawn correctly, otherwise 1 mark for two correct lines)
4. 18 × 3 = 54,
   so 18 × 30 = 54 × 10 = 540 **(1 mark)**
5. ```
     27        32         29
   ×  3      ×  5        ×  6
   ────      ────        ────
    81       160         174
    2         1            5
   ```
   (2 marks for all three correct, otherwise 1 mark for two correct)
6. One dragon scores 80 points.
   Two trolls score 35 × 2 = 70 points.
   Four goblins score 12 × 4 = 48 points.
   So she scores 80 + 70 + 48 = 198 points.
   (2 marks for the correct answer, otherwise 1 mark for a correct method)

Test 2 – pages 4-5

1. a) 8 b) 7 c) 11 d) 9
   (2 marks for all four correct, otherwise 1 mark for at least two correct)
2. a) 5 b) 7 c) 9 d) 8
   (2 marks for all four correct, otherwise 1 mark for at least two correct)
3. You can multiply numbers in any order.
   4 × 8 = 32 and 8 × 4 = 32, so 4 × 8 = 8 × 4 should be circled. **(1 mark)**

4. ```
      26
   ×   3
   ────
     78    (1 mark for both digits)
      1
   
      35
   ×   7
   ────
    245    (1 mark for both digits)
      3
   ```
5. 2 × 5 × 3 = 10 × 3 = 30
   6 × 2 × 10 = 12 × 10 = 120
   (1 mark for both correct)
6. ```
      68
   ×   6
   ────
    408    (1 mark)
      4
   ```
7. Each tube contains 5 + 4 = 9 tennis balls.
   So he buys 81 ÷ 9 = 9 tubes.
   9 tubes contain 9 × 5 = 45 yellow balls.
   (2 marks for the correct answer, otherwise 1 mark for a correct method)

Test 3 – pages 6-7

1. a) 36 and 66 should be circled.
   b) 14 and 42 should be circled.
   (1 mark for all correct)
2. a) 60 b) 120 c) 300 d) 330
   (2 marks for all four correct, otherwise 1 mark for at least two correct)
3. The calculations that should be circled are:
   16 ÷ 4, 36 ÷ 9, 28 ÷ 7
   (1 mark for all correct calculations circled and no others)
4. 14 × 10 = 140   370 × 10 = 3700
   20 × 100 = 2000   85 × 1000 = 85 000
   (2 marks for all four correct, otherwise 1 mark for at least two correct)
5. ```
      243                415
   ×    3             ×    4
   ────               ────
     729  (1 mark)    1660  (1 mark)
       1                 2
   ```
6. 72 × 6 = 70 × 6 + 2 × 6 = 420 + 12 = 432 legs
   (1 mark)
   56 × 8 = 50 × 8 + 6 × 8 = 400 + 48 = 448 legs
   (2 marks for the correct answer, otherwise 1 mark for a correct method)

5. Work out the answers to these calculations.

```
   3 1 0 6              4 2 8 8
 ×     4 2            ×     1 7
 ─────────            ─────────
```

/ 2 marks

6. Danesh says, "You can work out the volume of a cube by taking its side length and multiplying it by itself twice."

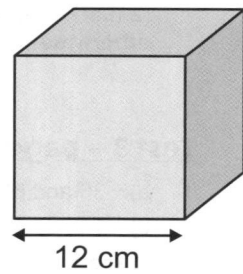

12 cm

Use his method to work out the volume of the cube above.

.... cm³

/ 2 marks

END OF TEST

/ 11

Test 12

Warm up

1. a) What number multiplied by 40 gives 240? ....

    b) What number divided by 9 gives 80? ....

    c) What number multiplied by 11 gives 440? ....

    2 marks

2. Fill in the gaps to complete these calculations.

    a) 815 ÷ .... = 0.815   b) .... × 10 = 78.4

    c) .... ÷ 100 = 1.22   d) 0.32 × .... = 320

    2 marks

3. Work out:

    204 × 36   861 × 92

    ....

    2 marks

4. Ella puts 1346 eggs into egg boxes.
    Each box can hold six eggs.

    How many whole boxes does she fill?

    .... boxes

    1 mark

5. Work out the answers to these calculations.

```
    3 0 2 7           4 3 1 1
  ×     2 1         ×     1 8
  ─────────         ─────────
```

2 marks

6. The ingredients below make one serving of pancakes.

135 g flour
2 eggs
300 ml milk

Rhys has a 1 kg bag of flour in the cupboard.

How much **more** flour does he need to make nine servings of pancakes?

.... g flour

2 marks

END OF TEST

/ 11

Test 11

Warm up

1. Work out the answers to these calculations.

   a) 2^3 = ...   b) 4^3 = ...

   1 mark

2. Fill in the gaps to complete these calculations.

   a) 8 × 11 = ... × 8   b) 12 × .... = 10 × 12

   c) 5 × 7 × 4 = 7 × ....   d) 9 × .... × 8 = 16 × 9

   2 marks

3. Work out the answers to these calculations.

   .... remainder: .... remainder: ......
   7 | 1 0 8 1   3 | 4 7 3 3

   2 marks

4. Write in the missing digits to make these calculations correct.

   ```
           9 ☐                    ☐ 7
       ×   2 4                ×   4 9
       -------                -------
         3 ☐ 2                  6 0 3
           1                        6
       + 1 8 6 0              + 2 6 ☐ 0
       -------                      2
         2 ☐ 3 2              -------
           1 1                  3 2 ☐ 3
                                    1
   ```

   2 marks

Test 11   22   © CGP — not to be photocopied

5. Fleur has 891 roses. She divides them into equal bunches of 6 roses.

   How many whole bunches of roses can she make?

   .... bunches

   1 mark

   Fleur also has 909 tulips. She wants to put them into vases.
   Each vase can hold 7 tulips.

   How many vases does she need to hold all of the tulips?

   .... vases

   1 mark

6. Padma puts a number into this number machine.
   She gets 864 out at the end.

   IN → Square the number → × 6 → OUT

   What number did she put into the machine?

   ....

   2 marks

   END OF TEST

   / 11